CHARLES DICKENS'S

Boots at the Holly Tree Inn

Peter Leigh

Published in association with The Basic Skills Agency

Hodder & Stoughton

A MEMBER OF THE HODDER HEADLINE GROUP

Acknowledgements
Cover: Ben Warner
Illustrations: Jim Eldridge
Photograph of Charles Dickens © The Hulton Getty Picture Collection Limited

Orders: please contact Bookpoint Ltd, 39 Milton Park, Abingdon, Oxon OX14 4TD. Telephone: (44) 01235 400414, Fax: (44) 01235 400454. Lines are open from 9.00–6.00, Monday to Saturday, with a 24 hour message answering service. Email address: orders@bookpoint.co.uk

British Library Cataloguing in Publication Data
A catalogue record for this title is available from The British Library

ISBN 0 340 74310 7

First published 1999
Impression number 10 9 8 7 6 5 4 3 2
Year   2005 2004 2003 2002 2001 2000 1999

Copyright © 1999 Peter Leigh

Typeset by Fakenham Photosetting Ltd, Fakenham, Norfolk.
Printed in Great Britain for Hodder & Stoughton Educational, a division of Hodder Headline Plc, 338 Euston Road, London NW1 3BH by Redwood Books Ltd, Trowbridge, Wiltshire.

About the author

Charles Dickens was born in 1812
and died in 1870.
He is one of our most popular writers,
and this is one of his most popular stories.

About the story

Charles Dickens was staying at an inn,
the Holly Tree Inn,
and was chatting to 'Boots'.
Boots wasn't his real name –
Cobbs was his real name –
but he was called Boots
because he cleaned everyone's boots and
shoes.

Dickens was asking him about his life,
what he had done and what he had seen ...

I expect you've been
to lots of different places.

Lord, yes! I've been everywhere.

And I expect you've seen a good deal?

Seen a good deal?
Why, of course I have.
It would be easier for me
to tell you what I haven't seen
than what I have.

What's the oddest thing you have seen?

The oddest thing?
Well, I don't know …
I can't think of the oddest thing …
unless it was a unicorn at a fair …

unicorn – a horse
with a horn on its
head.
It's from stories –
it's not a real animal.

1

I know,
suppose a young gentleman
just eight years old
was to run away to get married
with a fine young woman of seven.
Wouldn't you think that was odd?

I certainly would.

Well, sir, I saw them with my own eyes.
I even cleaned the shoes
they ran away in,
and they were so little
I couldn't get my hand in them.

You see, sir, Master Harry was an only child.
His father was a gentleman of spirit.
He had a will of his own
and a mind of his own.
He was very proud of Master Harry,
being his only child,
but he didn't spoil him neither.
He kept command over the child,

behaved like a child   and the child *was* a child.
And it's very much to be wished
that more of them were!

2

How do you know this
about Master Harry and his father?

I was the gardener there.
And while I was mowing and sweeping,
or weeding and pruning,
or this and that,
I got to know the ways of the family.

One morning Master Harry came to me, and
said,
'Cobbs, how do you spell Nora?'

I gave him my views
as to the spelling of the name,
and he took out his little knife,
and began carving it into the fence.

And the courage of the boy!
Bless you,
he would have thrown off his little hat,
tucked up his little sleeves,
and gone in at a lion, he would.

One day I was weeding,
and he stops by me,
along with little Nora.

'Cobbs,' he says, 'I like you.'

'Do you sir? I'm glad to hear it.'

'Yes I do, Cobbs.
Do you know why I like you, Cobbs?'

'No sir.'

'Because Nora likes you, Cobbs.'

'Indeed, sir? That's very nice, sir.'

'Nice, Cobbs?
It's better than
millions of the brightest diamonds
to be liked by Nora.
You shall be our Head Gardener
when we are married.'

And he tucks her under his arm,
in her little sky-blue mantle,
and walks away.

mantle is like
a shawl

5

Bless you sir,
it was better than a picture
to see them two babies
with their long, bright, curling hair,
their sparkling eyes,
and their beautiful light tread,
rambling about the garden,
deep in love.
Even the birds kept up with them,
singing just to please them.

Sometimes,
they would creep under the tulip tree,
and would sit there
with their arms round one another's necks,
and their soft cheeks touching,
reading about the Prince and the Dragon,
and the good fairy and the bad fairy,
and the King's fair daughter.
Sometimes I would hear them planning
about having a house in a forest,
keeping bees and a cow,
and living off milk and honey.

On the whole, sir,
just looking at those two babies
made me feel as if I was in love myself –
only I didn't exactly know who with.

Well sir, about that time,
I left Master Harry's father and came here,
to the Holly Tree Inn.

Why did you do that?

Well, sir, I was younger then,
and I wanted change.
I was going to seek my fortune.
And let me tell you,
I haven't found it yet.

Well, one summer's afternoon, here,
the coach drives up,
and out of the coach gets them two children.

governor – the boss

The Guard says to our governor,
'I can't quite make out these little passengers,
but the young gentlemen's words was,
that they was to be brought here.'

The young gentleman gets out,
hands his lady out,

something for himself – a tip

gives the Guard something for himself,
and says to our governor,
'We're to stop here tonight, please.
We'll need a sitting room and two bedrooms,
and lamb chops and cherry pudding for
two.'

And he tucks her under his arm,
in her little sky-blue mantle,
and walks into the house
much bolder than brass.

Well, everybody was amazed
when those two tiny creatures
all alone by themselves
marched into the inn!

They hadn't seen me,
so I told the governor who they were,
and where they came from.

'Cobbs,' says the governor,
'I must set off myself and get the parents.
You must keep your eye on them,
and humour them till I come back.
I'll be back tomorrow.'

'Sir,' says I, 'it shall be done directly.'

So I goes up to the sitting room,
and I finds Master Harry on
a e-normous sofa,
drying the eyes of Miss Nora.
Their little legs was entirely off the ground,
and I can't tell you
how small them children looked.

humour – keep
them happy.
Remember, there
were no phones,
cars or trains.

e-normous –
Dickens is trying to
write it like Boots
said it

'It's Cobbs! It's Cobbs!' cries Master Harry,
and he comes running to me
catching hold of my hand.
Miss Nora, she comes running to me
on the other side
and catching hold of my other hand,
they both jump for joy.

'I saw you getting out, sir,' says I.
'I thought it was you.
I thought I couldn't be mistaken
in your height and figure.
What's the object of your journey, sir?'

'We are going to be married, Cobbs,
at Gretna Green,' says the boy.
'We have run away on purpose.
Nora has been in rather low spirits, Cobbs,
but she'll be happy,
now we have found you to be our friend.'

'Thank you, sir, and thank you, miss,
for your good opinion.
Did you bring any luggage with you, sir?'

object here means purpose

Runaway English couples could get married in Scotland, and Gretna Green was very near the border.

parasol – a little
umbrella

You won't believe this,
but I give you my word of honour –
the lady had got a parasol, a smelling bottle,
a round and a half of cold buttered toast,
eight peppermint drops,
and a doll's hairbrush.

The gentleman had got about six yards of
string,
a knife,
three or four sheets of writing paper
folded up surprisingly small,
a orange,
and a mug with his name on it.

'What are your exact plans, sir?' says I.

'To go on,' says the boy –
and the courage of that boy
was something wonderful –
'to go on in the morning,
and be married tomorrow.'

'Just so, sir.
Would you mind, sir,
if I was to go with you?'

They both jumped for joy again,
and cried out, 'O yes, yes, Cobbs! Yes!'

'Well sir, if you don't mind me saying,
what I suggest is this –
I happen to know a pony, sir,
which, put in a cart that I could borrow,
would take you and Miss Nora,
to the end of your journey
in a very short space of time.
I'm not sure, sir,
that this pony will be free till tomorrow,
but even if you had to wait for him,
it might be worth your while.

account – bill

As to the small account here, sir,
in case you was to find yourself running at
all short,
that doesn't matter,
because I'm a part-owner of this inn,

you could pay
it back later

and it could stand over.'

Well, sir, they clapped their hands,
and jumped for joy again,
and called me 'Good Cobbs!' and 'Dear
Cobbs!',
and bent across me
to kiss one another in delight.

rascal – villain
Boots feels mean
because he is
pretending to
go along with them,
when really he
wants to keep them
at the inn until
the parents arrive.

And I felt the meanest rascal
for deceiving them,
that was ever born.

13

'Is there anything you want,
just at present, sir?' I says,
very ashamed of myself.

'We should like some cakes after dinner,'
says Master Harry,
'and two apples – and jam.
With dinner we should like to have
toast and water.
But Nora has been used

wine – juice

to half a glass of currant wine with pudding.'
And so have I.'

'It shall be ordered at the bar, sir,' I says.

Sir, I feel now just the same as I felt then,
that I wished with all my heart
there was some impossible place
where those two babies could make
an impossible marriage,
and live impossibly happy ever after.

However,
it couldn't be.

The women of the house –
every one of them, married or single,
really took to that boy
when they heard the story.
It was as much as could be done
to keep them from dashing into the room
and kissing him.
They climbed up all sorts of places,
at the risk of their lives,
to look at him through a pane of glass.
And they was seven deep at the key-hole.

In the evening, I went into the room
to see how the runaway couple was getting on.
The gentleman was in the window seat,
holding the lady in his arms.
She had tears upon her face,
and was lying, very tired and half asleep,
with her head upon his shoulder.

'Miss Nora tired, sir?'

'Yes, she is tired, Cobbs,
she is not used to being away from home,
and she has been in low spirits again.
Cobbs, do you think you could bring
a baked apple, please?'

'I beg your pardon, sir. What was it you …?'

'I think a baked apple would rouse her,
Cobbs.
She is very fond of them.'

Well, sir, I went and got the baked apple,
and the gentleman handed it to the lady,
and fed her with a spoon,
and took a little himself.

The lady was heavy with sleep, and rather
cross.
So I says,
'What should you think, sir, of bedtime?'

The gentleman said yes.
So the lady, in her sky-blue mantle,
went up the great staircase,
escorted by the gentleman.
The gentleman embraced her at the door,
and retired to his own room,
where I locked him in.

embraced – kissed
retired – went to bed

At breakfast next morning
they had toast and jam.
They asked me about the pony.

I don't mind telling you, sir,
it was as much as I could do
to look them two young things in the face.

like a Trojan –
this was a saying
of the time.
It just means 'a lot'.
clipped – having its
coat cut

Still, sir, I went on lying like a Trojan.
I told them that unfortunately,
the pony was half clipped,
and couldn't be took out in that state.
But he'd be finished clipping during today,
and by tomorrow morning the cart would be
ready.

Looking back on it, sir,
I think that Miss Nora was beginning to
give in.
She hadn't had her hair curled
when she went to bed,
and she didn't seem up to brushing it herself,
and it kept getting into her eyes.

But nothing put out Master Harry.

'Cobbs,' he said brightly,
'are there any good walks nearby?'

'Yes, sir. There's Love Lane.'

'Get away with you, Cobbs!'
(that was the boy's very words)
'You're joking.'

'Begging your pardon, sir,
there really is a Love Lane.
And a pleasant walk it is,
and I shall be glad to show it
to yourself and Miss Nora.'

'Nora, dear,' says Master Harry,
'we really ought to see Love Lane.
Put on your bonnet,
and we will go there with Cobbs.'

So, I took them down Love Lane
to the water meadows,
and they was telling me
how they were going to give me
two thousand pounds a year as Head
Gardener
because I was so true a friend to them.

And then when we got there,
Master Harry near drowned himself
getting a water lily for Miss Nora –
nothing scared that boy.

Well, sir, they was tired out,
all being so new and strange to them.
They was as tired as tired could be.
And they laid down on a bank of daisies,
like the babes in the wood, and fell asleep.

I don't know, sir – perhaps you do –
what it does to a man,
to see them two pretty babies
lying there in the clear still sunny day.
Lord, when you come to think of yourself,
and what a game you have been up to,
ever since you was in your own cradle,
and what a poor sort of chap you are after
all –
that's what gets to a man!
Don't you see, sir?

Well, sir, they woke up at last,
and one thing was clear to me,
that Miss Nora was starting to lose her
temper.
She said that Master Harry was 'teasing' her,
and when he says,
'Nora, I don't "tease" you',
she tells him, 'Yes, you do!
And I want to go home!'

A little chicken and bread and butter
pudding
cheered Miss Nora up a little.
And, I can tell you sir,
she was keener on the currants in the
pudding
than on the voice of love!

However, Master Harry kept up,
and his noble heart was as fond as ever.

Miss Nora turned very sleepy about dusk,
and began to cry.
Therefore Miss Nora went off to bed
as per yesterday,
ditto – the same   and Master Harry ditto.

About eleven or twelve at night,
back comes the governor in a coach
along with Master Harry's father
and an elderly lady.

Master Harry's father says,
'We are very grateful, sir,
for your kind care of our little children.
Please, where is my boy?'

The governor says,
'Cobbs has the dear child in charge, sir.'

Then Master Harry's father says,
'Ah Cobbs! I am glad to see you.
I understood you was here.'

'Yes sir. Your most obedient, sir.'

Dickens has
missed out
'servant',
to show
the way Cobbs talks.

And I takes Master Harry's father
along to Master Harry's room.
And I adds, as I'm unlocking the door,
'I beg your pardon, sir.
I hope you're not angry with Master Harry.
For Master Harry is a fine boy, sir,

credit and honour –
will be worthy
of you

and will do you credit and honour.'
But he only says, 'No, Cobbs.
No, my good fellow. Thank you.'

And, with the door open,
he goes in,
and goes up to the bedside.
He bends gently down,
and kisses the little sleeping face.

Then he stands looking at it for a minute,
looking very much like it,
and then he gently shakes the little shoulder.

'Harry, my dear boy! Harry!'

Master Harry starts up and looks at his Pa.
Looks at me too.

mite – tiny animal

Such is the honour of that mite,
that he looks at me,
to see whether he has got me into trouble.

'I am not angry, my child.
I only want you to dress yourself
and come home.'

'Yes, Pa.'

Master Harry dresses himself quick.

'Please may I' – the spirit of that little boy –
'please, dear Pa – may I –
kiss Nora before I go?'

'You may, my child.'

So he takes Master Harry in his hand,
and I leads the way with the candle,
to the other bedroom,
where the elderly lady is seated by the bed,
and poor little Miss Nora is fast asleep.

There, the father lifts the boy up to the
pillow,
and he lays his little face down
next to the little warm face of Miss Nora,
and gently draws it to him.
It's a sight so touching
that one of the maids,
who are peeping through the door,
cries out, 'It's a shame to part them.'

Well, sir, that's about all there is.
Master Harry's father drove away
in the carriage,
having hold of Master Harry's hand,
and the elderly lady and Miss Nora went off
the next day.

Now, sir, let me ask you,
whether you agree with me on two things –
first, that there are not many couples
on their way to be married,
who are half as innocent as them two
children –
second, that it would be a very good thing
for a great many couples
on their way to be married,
if they could only be stopped in time,
and brought back separate!